Published in 2023 by OH!
An imprint of Welbeck Non-Fiction Limited, part of Welbeck Publishing
Group. Offices in London, 20 Mortimer Street, London W1T 3JW, and
Sydney, 205 Commonwealth Street, Surry Hills 2010.
www.welbeckpublishing.com

A CIP catalogue record for this book is available from the British Library.

ISBN 978-1-83861-168-2

Publisher: Lisa Dyer
Compilation and writing: Katie Hewett
Design: Lucy Palmer
Production: Felicity Awdry

Printed and bound in Dubai

10 9 8 7 6 5 4 3 2 1

YOU GOT THIS

MOTIVATIONAL QUOTES
FOR FIERCE FEMALES

CONTENTS

However strong and capable we may be, there are always times when things don't go the way we want them to, when we don't feel good enough and when things get too much.
You Got This is a collection of motivational slogans and quotes, by women — from CEOs and superstars, athletes and activists, authors and heroines — to celebrate female power and potential and give you the tools to get back on track. The five chapters look at different areas where the right words could give you the right boost at the right time.

Self-Belief Is Your Superpower! encourages you to have faith in your abilities to overcome the setbacks you may be facing, to bounce back from any failures and to keep striving upwards. Celebrate & Honour You is for the times you lose sight of the wonderful person you see in the mirror and to remind you to celebrate and appreciate yourself. You're the Boss! is about pushing yourself to achieve your goals, to fight your corner and speak your mind. Choose Your Battles is about balancing work and life and not punishing yourself for the choices you have to make. Finally, Persist & Insist will motivate you to stay focused and positive so that you can rise to challenges and get to where you want to be.

Remember that you are enough; you are amazing. If you put your mind to it, you can find the will to overcome fears, discover your dreams and take whatever life throws at you.

YOU GOT THIS!

1

SELF-BELIEF IS YOUR SUPERPOWER!

Believe it! You have infinite potential. You are a brilliant and unique human being with the talents, achievements, personality and get-up-and-go needed to face any challenge.
And yes, you might have a few minor flaws, but you have to have something to work on.
No one's perfect!

Having faith in your own abilities and hope for the future will help you overcome any obstacles in your path. When you find the going gets tough, think of all your past triumphs and celebrate them. Remember that you've gone through far worse before and you've not only survived but thrived.

66

I don't have to be perfect. All I have to do is show up and enjoy the messy, imperfect and beautiful journey of my life.

99

Kerry Washington, actor

Make the most of yourself by fanning the tiny, inner sparks of possibility into flames of achievement.

Golda Meir, politician

> "
>
> **We think, mistakenly, that success is the result of the amount of time we put in at work, instead of the quality of time we put in.**
>
> "

Arianna Huffington, co-founder and editor-in-chief of *The Huffington Post*

"

Where there's hope, there's life. It fills us with fresh courage and makes us strong again.

"

Anne Frank, *The Diary of a Young Girl* (1947)

66

Optimism is a happiness magnet. If you stay positive, good things and good people will be drawn to you.

99

Mary Lou Retton, gymnast

"Don't push your weaknesses, play with your STRENGTHS."

Jennifer Lopez, singer and actor

You are awesome.

I'm not suggesting you be boastful. No one likes that in men or women. But I am suggesting that believing in yourself is the first necessary step to coming even close to achieving your potential.

Sheryl Sandberg, businesswoman and philanthropist

"

... to free us from the expectations of others, to give us back to ourselves – there lies the great, singular power of self-respect.

"

Joan Didion, writer, *Vogue* 1961

I'm actively working hard on learning to appreciate yourself no matter what. If what someone else says can easily derail you, it means your sense of self isn't that firmly established in the first place. It's an inside job.

You're beautiful and worthy and totally unique. People insult each other based on their own insecurities — even though it may feel personal, it really never is. Really. Seriously.

Emma Stone, actor,
Seventeen, May 2014

"

Every individual matters. Every individual has a role to play. Every individual makes a difference.

"

Jane Goodall, author and naturalist

Some women choose to follow men, and some women choose to follow their dreams. If you're wondering which way to go, remember that your career will never wake up and tell you that it doesn't love you anymore.

Lady Gaga, singer and actor

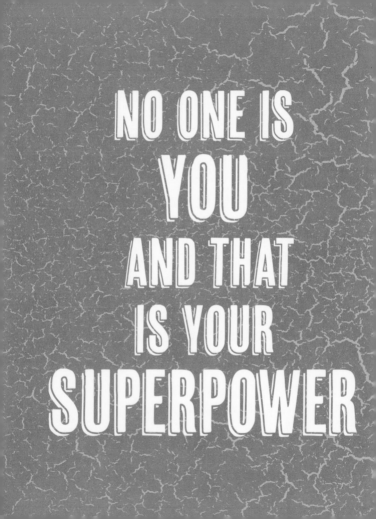

Women are leaders everywhere you look — from the CEO who runs a Fortune 500 company to the housewife who raises her children and heads her household. Our country was built by strong women, and we will continue to break down walls and defy stereotypes.

Nancy Pelosi, politician, *Glamour*, January 2007

"

I'm BETTER for all the things that have happened to me, the good and the bad.

"

Julia Roberts, actor

Never underestimate the power of dreams and the influence of the human spirit. We are all the same in this notion: the potential for greatness lives within each of us.

Wilma Rudolph, athlete

The important thing to realize is that no matter what people's opinions may be, they're only just that – people's opinions. You have to believe in your heart what you know to be true about yourself and let that be that.

Mary J. Blige, singer-songwriter

66

You can't be that kid standing at the top of the waterslide, overthinking it. You have to go down the chute.

99

Tina Fey, actor and comedian

"

Doubt kills more dreams than failure ever will.

"

Suzy Kassem, poet

We often don't like to look at certain things because we're not feeling grateful, but we should dare to look in the mirror and make an active choice to move on, forgive and forget, and be grateful for the things we have.

Michaela Coel, actor and screenwriter

66

Success is a state of mind. If you want success, start thinking of yourself as a success.

99

Joyce Brothers, psychologist

"

You cannot live your life looking at yourself from someone else's point of view.

"

Penélope Cruz, actor

"

I choose to make the rest of my life the BEST of my life.

"

Louise Hay, author

I wanted a perfect ending. Now I've learned, the hard way, that some poems don't rhyme, and some stories don't have a clear beginning, middle, and end. Life is about not knowing, having to change, taking the moment and making the best of it, without knowing what's going to happen next. Delicious ambiguity.

Gilda Radner, actor,
It's Always Something (1989)

"

Whatever it is that you think you want to do, and whatever it is that you think stands between you and that, stop making excuses.

YOU CAN DO ANYTHING.

"

Katia Beauchamp,
co-founder and CEO of Birchbox

" She believed she could, so she did. "

R. S. Grey, author, *Scoring Wilder* (2014)

If you keep waiting for the right time, it may never happen. Sometimes you have to make the most of the time you have.

Priya Ardis, author

66

You can never be the best. The only thing you can be the best at is developing YOURSELF.

99

Natalie Portman, actor

There are going to be moments where you struggle and you ask yourself, 'Do I deserve to be here? Am I really good enough for this position? Am I as good as the person I'm comparing myself to?' I want to tell you something: You are SO good; you are SO okay. And accept all of the good that comes your way because you deserve it, because it was written for you ...

Noor Tagouri, journalist, *Teen Vogue*
Commencement 2020

66

You may be the only person left who believes in you, but it's enough. It takes just one star to pierce a universe of darkness. Never give up.

99

Richelle E. Goodrich, author

" The only way to get what you really want is to let go of what you don't want. "

Iyanla Vanzant, motivational speaker

... just because you fail once, it doesn't mean you're going to fail at everything. Keep trying, hold on, and always, always, always believe in yourself because if you don't, then who will? So, keep your head high, keep your chin up, and most importantly, keep smiling because life's a beautiful thing and there's so much to smile about.

Marilyn Monroe, actor

66

It is our CHOICES that show what we truly are, far more than our abilities.

99

J.K. Rowling, author

66

If you doubt you can accomplish something, then you can't accomplish it. You have to have confidence in your ability, and then be tough enough to follow through.

99

Rosalynn Carter, former First Lady of the USA

"

If you don't believe in yourself, nobody else will. Have a little more CONFIDENCE.

"

Cathy Moriarty, actor

66

The only one who can tell you 'you can't win' is YOU, and YOU don't have to listen.

99

Jessica Ennis-Hill, athlete

"

I've finally stopped running away from myself. Who else is there better to be?

"

Goldie Hawn, actor

66

I know what it's like to feel that fear and the need of affirmation and appreciation. To build confidence in yourself is the toughest thing.

99

Shakira, singer

Be your

STRONGEST

when you feel

at your weakest

66
You control your own wins and losses.
99

Maria Sharapova, tennis player

" "

Be strong, be fearless, be beautiful. And believe that anything is possible when you have the right people there to support YOU.

" "

Misty Copeland, ballerina

66

Think of yourself as your own pet, and be gently fascinated and amused by the mad-ass crazy shit that's happening to you as you march on down life's long path.

99

Caitlin Moran, journalist

You
are
ENOUGH
A thousand times
ENOUGH

"

THIS LIFE
IS MINE ALONE.
So, I have stopped
asking people
for directions to
places they've
never been.

Glennon Doyle, author

"

... there are two kinds of people, those who do the work and those who take the credit ... Try to be in the first group; there is less competition there.

"

Indira Gandhi, politician

66

I think the best way to have confidence is not to allow everyone else's insecurities to be your own.

99

Jessie J, singer

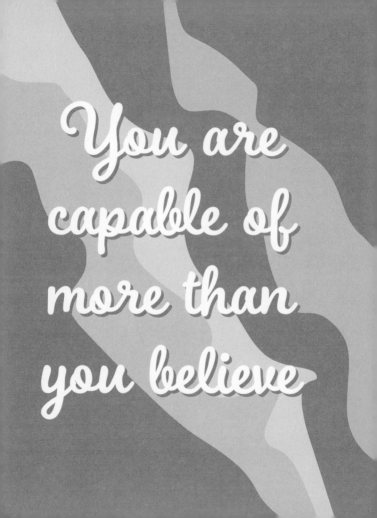

CELEBRATE &
HONOUR YOU

Give yourself a round of applause! You are amazing and everyone needs to know it, especially you. Learning to love, respect and appreciate yourself will give you the confidence, self-worth and positivity to kill it each and every day. Even more importantly, self-love will help you recognize the boundaries you need in order for you to best BE YOU and DO YOU. Knowing yourself – the triggers that tip you over the edge or the toxic self-talk that limits you, as well as the things that energize and motivate you – will help you become more resilient and create a balanced life.

Women in particular need to keep an eye on their physical and mental health, because if we're scurrying to and from appointments and errands, we don't have a lot of time to take care of ourselves. We need to do a better job of putting ourselves higher on our own 'to do' list.

Michelle Obama,
lawyer, author and former First Lady of the USA

66

Once you figure out who you are and what you love about yourself, it all kind of falls into place.

99

Jennifer Aniston, actor

66

The most important relationship in your life is with yourself. Because no matter what happens, you will always BE YOURSELF.

99

Diane von Furstenberg, fashion designer

Be happy with being you. Love your flaws. Own your quirks. And know that you are just as perfect as anyone else, exactly as you are.

Ariana Grande, singer

"
Never dull your shine for somebody else.
"

Tyra Banks, model and presenter

There's something so special about a woman who dominates in a man's world. It takes a certain grace, strength, intelligence, fearlessness, and the nerve to never take no for an answer.

Rihanna, singer and businesswoman

Behind every **SUCCESSFUL woman** is **HERSELF**

People respond well to those that are sure of what they want. What people hate most is indecision. Even if I'm completely unsure, I'll pretend I know exactly what I'm talking about and make a decision.

Anna Wintour, *Vogue* editor

66

If you're presenting yourself with confidence, you can pull off pretty much anything.

99

Katy Perry, singer

YOU ARE THE LOVE. YOU ARE THE ETHEREAL HAND WATERING YOUR CELESTIAL FLOWERS. YOU ARE THE BLISS.

There are clouds moving in and out of your lungs; you are the bees and you are the honeycomb and you are this honey in your own jar and then atop your own tongue!

C. JoyBell C., author

66

Talk to yourself like you would to someone you love.

99

Brené Brown,
academic and author

66

To lose confidence in one's body is to lose confidence in oneself.

99

Simone de Beauvoir,
philosopher, writer and activist

66

Your words have so much power. Every day, if you tell yourself, I LOVE YOU, if you give yourself one word of validation, it will change your mind.

99

Ashley Graham, model and presenter

66

Feeling confident, being comfortable in your skin – that's what really makes you beautiful.

99

Bobbi Brown, businesswoman

The most important thing is to be honest about yourself. Secrets weigh heavy and it's when you try to keep everything to yourself that it becomes a burden. You waste energy agonizing when you could be living your life and realizing your dreams.

Nicola Adams, boxer

"

It's all about accepting yourself the way you are. If you want to work towards a better you in whatever regards ... do it. But you're okay just the way you are today.

"

Tess Holliday, model

"

There is no such thing as ugly. That's a word that doesn't really enter my vocabulary. If there's any definition to being perfect, you're PERFECT AT BEING YOURSELF.

Zendaya, singer and actor

"

I'm a normal person, just a lot smaller. I get on with it. Everybody should do that. You only live once and you need to enjoy life, to go out and achieve whatever you want to.

"

Ellie Simmonds, Paralympian

66

If you focus on the inside, you'll feel just as great about the outside. I feel attractive when I'm doing good and helping people.

99

Keke Palmer, actor

"

To love yourself as you are is a miracle, and to seek yourself is to have found yourself, for now. And now is all we have, and love is who we are.

"

Anne Lamott, author

66

I've made peace with the fact that the things that I thought were weaknesses or flaws were just me. I LIKE THEM.

Sandra Bullock, actor

I've finally recognized my body for what it is: a personality-delivery system, designed expressly to carry my character from place to place, now and in the years to come.

Anna Quindlen, author

Confidence comes with maturity, being more accepting of yourself.

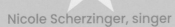

Nicole Scherzinger, singer

66

Along with age comes
MORE CONFIDENCE,
so it kind of
works out.

99

Leslie Mann, actor

I believe in going with the flow. I don't believe in fighting against the flow.

You ride on your river and you go with the tides and the flow.

But it has to be your river, not someone else's. Everyone has their own river, and you don't need to swim, float, sail on theirs.

C. JoyBell C., author

"Love yourself first and everything else falls into line. You really have to love yourself to get anything done in this world.

Lucille Ball,
actor

Regardless of how you feel inside, always try to look like a winner. Even if you are behind, a sustained look of control and confidence can give you a mental edge that results in victory.

Diane Arbus, photographer

66

Don't forget to tell yourself positive things daily! You must love yourself internally to glow externally.

99

Hannah Bronfman, DJ and influencer

66

In order to love who you are, you cannot hate the experiences that shaped you.

99

Andrea Dykstra, author

" Keep taking time for yourself until you're you again. "

Lalah Delia, writer

"You change the world by being yourself."

Yoko Ono, artist and singer

66

If you are happy, you can give happiness. If you don't love yourself and if you are unhappy with yourself, you can't give anything else but that.

99

Gisele Bündchen, model

Love yourself enough to set boundaries. Your time and energy are precious. You get to choose how you use it. You teach people how to treat you by deciding what you will and won't accept.

Anna Taylor, author

"

Beauty is when you can appreciate yourself. When you love yourself, that's when you're most BEAUTIFUL.

"

Zoë Kravitz, actor

"

Breathe and don't try and be perfect.

"

Nicole Kidman, actor

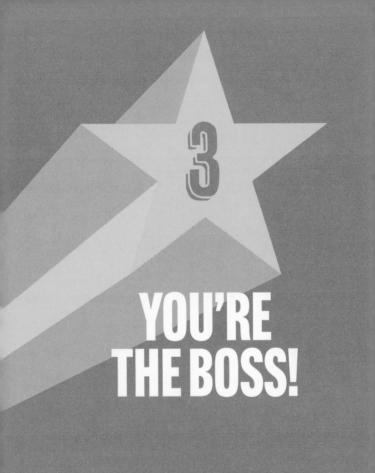

3

YOU'RE THE BOSS!

You are the kick-ass boss of your life and don't forget it. No one can do you like you. Stand strong in your convictions, be guided by your passion and take the steps you need towards success, whatever that means for you. If you're trying to figure it all out, think about what you want to do with your one wild and precious life and give it all you've got. Don't forget that you are allowed to change your mind and change direction. You're the only one in the driving seat.

❝

You have to balance YOUR PASSIONS, not your time.

❞

Lisa Sugar,
founder and president of Popsugar

You will never feel truly satisfied by work until you are satisfied by life.

Heather Schuck, author of
The Working Mom Manifesto (2013)

"

Just don't give up trying to do what you really want to do. Where there is love and inspiration, I don't think you can go wrong.

"

Ella Fitzgerald, singer

You make a choice: continue living your life feeling muddled in this abyss of self-misunderstanding, or you find your identity independent of it. You draw your own box.

Meghan, Duchess of Sussex, *Good Housekeeping*, October 2022

"

You can't just sit there and wait for people to give you that golden dream. You've got to get out there and make it happen for yourself.

"

Diana Ross, singer

66

What gives you pleasure and joy? Let those be the things that lead you forward in life.

99

Julianne Moore, actor

The success of every woman should be the inspiration to another. We should raise each other up. Make sure you're very courageous: be strong, be extremely kind, and above all be humble.

Serena Williams, tennis player,
Time magazine, 2016

The distance between your DREAMS and reality is called ACTION

"

Just remember, you can do anything you set your mind to, but it takes action, perseverance and facing your fears.

"

Gillian Anderson, actor

Every decision I have made – from changing jobs, to changing partners, to changing homes – has been taken with trepidation. I have not ceased being fearful, but I have ceased to let fear control me. I have accepted fear as a part of life, specifically the fear of change, the fear of the unknown, and I have gone ahead despite the pounding in the heart that says: turn back, turn back, you'll die if you venture too far ... I have learned, in short, to trust myself. Not to eradicate fear but to go on in spite of fear.

Erica Jong, *What Do Women Want?* (2007)

"

Be bold, be brave enough to be YOUR TRUE SELF.

"

Queen Latifah, rapper and actor

66

The most effective way to do it is TO DO IT.

99

Amelia Earhart, aviator

"

What is important is to believe in something so strongly that you're never discouraged.

"

Salma Hayek, actor

Other women who are killing it should motivate you, thrill you, challenge you and inspire you, rather than threaten you and make you feel like you're immediately being compared to them.

Taylor Swift, singer-songwriter

I always did something I was a little not ready to do. I think that's how you grow. When there's that moment of 'Wow, I'm not really sure I can do this,' and you push through those moments, that's when you have a **BREAKTHROUGH.**

Marissa Mayer,
businesswoman and investor

66

Take criticism seriously, but not personally. If there is truth or merit in the criticism, try to learn from it. Otherwise, let it roll right off you.

99

Hillary Clinton, politician and diplomat

I just want you to spend 30 minutes a day doing something to help you become the person that you secretly would love to be, to do the job that you secretly would love to do, because if I can tell you anything, it's that you can actually do it — and not in a cheesy, follow-your-dreams way. Believe in yourself, even though that's true, it's more just that what you want to do is possible, because there are people who are doing it and it was impossible for them at one time too.

Tomi Adeyemi, author,
Teen Vogue Commencement 2002

If you try anything, if you try to lose weight, or to improve yourself, or to love, or to make the world a better place, you have already achieved something wonderful, before you even begin. Forget failure. If things don't work out the way you want, hold your head up high and be proud. And try again. And again. And again!

Sarah Dessen, author,
Keeping the Moon (1999)

"

Get comfortable with being uncomfortable!

"

Jillian Michaels, personal trainer

66

The more you can be authentic, the happier you're going to be, and life will work itself around that.

99

Melinda Gates

Be the kind of woman that makes other women want to up their game

> **Don't waste a single second. Just move forward as fast as you can, and go for it.**

Rebecca Woodcock,
co-founder of Cake Health

"

Many women live like it's a dress rehearsal. Ladies, the curtain is up AND YOU'RE ON.

"

Mikki Taylor, lifestyle author

"

I learned to always take on things I'd never done before. Growth and comfort do not coexist.

"

Ginni Rometty,
former chair, president and CEO of IBM

"

Define SUCCESS on your own terms, achieve it by your own rules, and build a life you're PROUD to live.

"

Anne Sweeney,
former co-chair of Disney Media

I'm willing to be seen.

I'm willing to speak up.

I'm willing to keep going.

I'm willing to listen
to what others have to say.

I'm willing to go to bed each
night at peace with myself.

I'm willing to be my biggest,
bestest, most powerful self.

Emma Watson, actor

We
don't grow
when things
are easy,
we grow
when we face
challenges.

❝

I was always looking outside myself for strength and confidence, but it comes from within. It is there all the time.

❞

Anna Freud, psychoanalyst

66

Never set limits, go after your dreams, don't be afraid to push the boundaries. And laugh a lot – it's good for you!

99

Paula Radcliffe, athlete

66

**In life, just find
something you LOVE and
make it your life.
That is the only way
to be successful.
LOVE WHAT YOU DO.**

99

Hannah Cockcroft, Paralympian

"

YOU ONLY GET ONE LIFE.

I've just made a decision to change things a bit and spend what's left of mine looking after ME for a change.

"

Bridget, *Bridget Jones's Diary*
by Helen Fielding (1996)

A new job
is not a new
beginning.
It is a path
to create a
new ending.

"

Perfectionism is a lost cause. Focus your energy on being the BEST YOU CAN BE.

"

Domonique Bertolucci, author

4

CHOOSE YOUR BATTLES

You can fight the good fight but you can't fight ALL the fights! Learn to recognize when something isn't working for you, isn't worth your energy or you are following someone else's lead that isn't a good fit for you. Letting go and learning to say no is just as important as achieving your goals. Life balance comes down to choices and they are all yours to make – no one else's. And you have many more choices than you think you have.

It's a myth that you can't have it all. You can have it all – just maybe not all at the same time.

Eva Longoria, actor

If I am accepting a prestigious award, I am missing my baby's first swim lesson. If I am at my daughter's debut in her school musical, I am missing Sandra Oh's last scene ever being filmed at *Grey's Anatomy*. If I am succeeding at one, I am inevitably failing at the other. That is the trade-off. That is the Faustian bargain one makes with the devil that comes with being a powerful working woman who is also a powerful mother. You never feel a hundred per cent OK; you never get your sea legs; you are always a little nauseous. Something is always lost.

Shonda Rhimes,
screenwriter, producer and author

I think moms, single or not, put a lot of pressure on ourselves trying to balance it all. It's NEVER going to be perfectly balanced – the sooner you know this, the sooner you can relieve some of the pressure you put on yourself.

Denise Richards, actor and TV personality

Telling women that some women 'have it all' only makes others feel less-than. I think we all have different struggles and issues ... My mother once said to me, "There's a time to mother, a time to be single, a time to work, a time to volunteer, a time to pray, a time to be active, a time to be, a time to do, a time to talk to yourself, and a time to be quiet." ... Get up, be grateful, try to center yourself, and try to do your best that day.

Maria Shriver, journalist and author

"

Balance is not better time management, but better boundary management. Balance means making choices and enjoying those choices.

"

Betsy Jacobson, business consultant

"

You can't have everything you want, but you can have the things that really matter to you.

"

Marissa Mayer, businesswoman and investor

66

When you're clear about your purpose and your priorities, you can painlessly discard whatever does not support these, whether it's clutter in your cabinets or commitments on your calendar.

99

Victoria Moran, *Lit from Within* (2001)

Victory isn't all that matters. Making the best use of your time is.

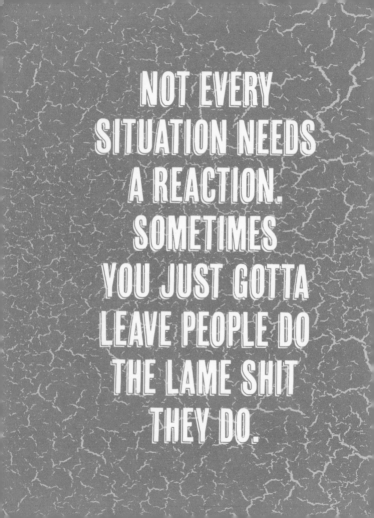

66

Don't waste words on people who deserve your silence. Sometimes the most powerful thing you can say is nothing at all.

99

Mandy Hale, author and blogger

When you notice someone does something toxic the first time, don't wait for the second time before you address it or cut them off.

Many survivors are used to the "wait and see" tactic which only leaves them vulnerable to a second attack. As your boundaries get stronger, the wait time gets shorter. You never have justify your intuition.

Shahida Arabi, author of *The Smart Girl's Guide to Self-Care*

> **If you want to have enough to give to others, you will need to take care of yourself first. A tree that refuses water and sunlight for itself can't bear fruit ...**

Emily Maroutian, author of *In Case Nobody Told You* (2018)

As all entrepreneurs know, you live and die by your ability to prioritize. You must focus on the most important mission-critical tasks each day and night, and then share, delegate, delay or skip the rest.

Jessica Jackley,
mentor to The Girl Effect Accelerator

"You don't get time. You create time.

"

Sanhita Baruah,
author of *The Art of Letting Go*

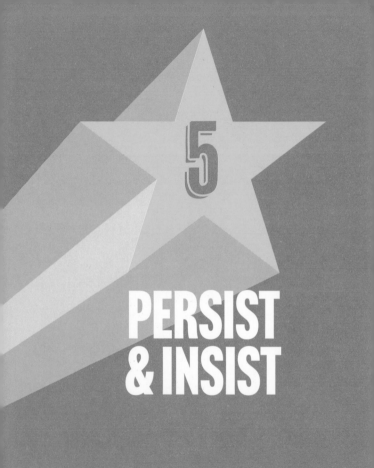

5

PERSIST
& INSIST

What is the thing that can push you through when you're hitting a wall? Your naturally given persistence and determination! Humans have a unique ability to have a vision and set on a path towards it, and even though the road may be challenging and you can't see the fruits of your labour quite yet, perserverance – the act of getting up each day and striving – will win out. Learn how to say NO to the haters and naysayers and insist on your voice and vision being heard.

66

When we show up, act boldly, and practice the best ways to be wrong, we fail forward. No matter where we end up, we've grown from where we began.

99

Stacey Abrams, politician

"

The question is not whether you have the money. It is whether you have the hustle. There's a difference!

"

Nicky Verd,
author of *Disrupt Yourself or Be Disrupted*

No matter what you're going through, there's a light at the end of the tunnel and it may seem hard to get to it, but you can do it and just keep working towards it and you'll find the positive side of things.

Demi Lovato, singer

66

You do not find the happy life. You make it.

99

Camilla Eyring Kimball, author

IT'S NOT ABOUT
BEING THE BEST.
IT'S ABOUT BEING
BETTER THAN
YOU WERE
YESTERDAY.

"

You are never too old to set another goal or to dream a new dream.

"

Malala Yousafzai, education activist

"

Champions keep playing until they get it right.

"

Billie Jean King,
tennis player

66

When one door of happiness closes, another opens; but often we look so long at the closed door that we do not see the one which has been opened for us.

99

Helen Keller, disability rights advocate

66

When I'm not feeling my best I ask myself, 'What are you gonna do about it?' I use the negativity to fuel the transformation into a better me.

99

Beyoncé Knowles,
singer and businesswoman

Persistence pushes me to be bold and seek out the opportunities I've wanted. It starts by envisioning what you want, no matter how big or small, and believing that you can achieve it.

Belinda Johnson, former CEO of Airbnb

66

The question isn't who's going to LET me; it's who's going to STOP me.

99

Ayn Rand

your

only

limit

is you

66

Sometimes you can do everything right and things will still go wrong. The key is to never stop doing right.

99

Angie Thomas, author

Be
STRONGER
than
your
excuses

"

Courage doesn't always roar. Sometimes courage is the quiet voice at the end of the day saying, I will try again tomorrow.

"

Mary Anne Radmacher, author

66

It's never too late to take a leap of faith and see what happens – and to be BRAVE in life.

99

Jane Fonda, actor and activist

"

Life comes with many challenges. The ones that should not scare us are the ones we can take on and take control of.

"

Angelina Jolie, actor

66

Do every job you're in like you're going to do it for the rest of your life, and demonstrate that ownership of it.

99

Mary Barra, CEO of General Motors

"

We may have doubts, but we control the present. We always have the choice to move forward with hope and confidence.

"

Teri Hatcher, actor

Life is not easy for any of us. But what of that? We must have perseverance and above all confidence in ourselves. We must believe that we are gifted for something, and that this thing must be attained.

Marie Curie, physicist and chemist

Don't let the fear of failing hold you back. You never know how far you can go if you don't take the first step.

"

It's amazing what you can get if you quietly, clearly and **AUTHORITATIVELY DEMAND IT.**

Meryl Streep, actor,
Golden Globes, 2007

"In the end, some of your greatest pains become your greatest strengths."

Drew Barrymore, actor

"

There may be days when you'll say to yourself, 'I can't. I literally can't even.' BUT YOU CAN! YOU CAN EVEN!

"

Katie Couric,
journalist, author and presenter

"

Don't be intimidated by what you don't know. That can be your GREATEST STRENGTH and ensure that you do things differently from everyone else.

"

Sara Blakely, founder of Spanx

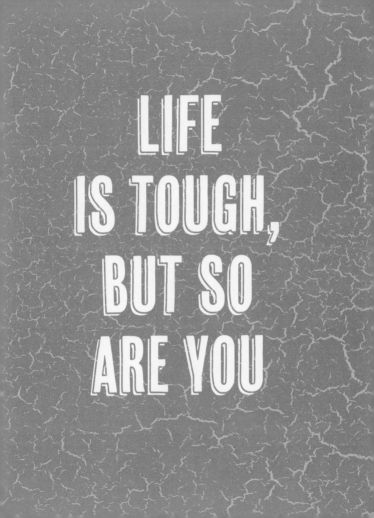

66

Doubt can motivate you, so don't be afraid of it. Confidence and doubt are at two ends of the scale, and you need both. They balance each other out.

99

Barbra Streisand, singer and actor

"Never put an age limit on your dreams."

Dara Torres, swimmer

66

I don't run away from a challenge because I am afraid. Instead, I run toward it because the only way to escape fear is to trample it beneath your feet.

99

Nadia Comăneci, gymnast

66

You always have to carry on. And you can, because you have to.

99

Kate Winslet, actor

66

A really strong woman accepts the war she went through and is ennobled by her scars.

99

Carly Simon, singer

"

It is never too late to be what you might have been.

"

George Eliot, author

" When life gives you lemons, squirt someone in the eye. "

Cathy Guisewite, cartoonist

Sometimes, the worst moment of your entire career can be the catalyst for a new chapter, a new project, a brilliant new invention or system – maybe the best work you've ever done.

Alexandra Franzen,
You're Going to Survive (2022)

66

When nothing is sure, everything is possible.

99

Margaret Drabble, author

Life's
failures
are
stepping stones
to
SUCCESS

Life doesn't always present you with the perfect opportunity at the perfect time. Opportunities come when you least expect them, or when you're not ready for them. Rarely are opportunities presented to you in the perfect way, in a nice little box with a yellow bow on top: here, open it, it's perfect — you'll love it!

Opportunities, the good ones, they're messy and confusing and hard to recognize. They're risky. They challenge you. But things happen so fast because our world is changing so much. You have to make decisions without perfect information.

Susan Wojcicki, CEO of YouTube, Johns Hopkins University speech, 2014

NEVER GIVE UP,
for that is just the
place and time
that the tide
will turn.

Harriet Beecher Stowe,
author and abolitionist